New Car Carriers
1900 - 1998
Photo Album

Donald F. Wood

Iconografix
Photo Album Series

Iconografix Inc. exists to preserve history through the publication of notable photographic archives and the list of titles under the Iconografix imprint is constantly growing. Transportation enthusiasts should be on the Iconografix mailing list and are invited to write and ask for a catalog, free of charge.

Authors and editors in the field of transportation history are invited to contact the Editorial Department at Iconografix, Inc., PO Box 446, Hudson, WI 54016. We require a minimum of 120 photographs per subject. We prefer subjects narrow in focus, e.g., a specific model, railroad, or racing venue. Photographs must be of high-quality, suited to large format reproduction.

Iconografix
PO Box 446
Hudson, Wisconsin 54016 USA

Library of Congress Card Number: 98-75272

ISBN 1-882256-98-0

99 00 01 02 03 04 05 5 4 3 2 1

Printed in the United States of America

Cover and book design by Shawn Glidden
Edited by Dylan Frautschi

DEDICATION

Phill Baumgarten (who was once in the business)

Acknowledgments

Several people have helped over the years with information and materials on this topic. They include: Phill Baumgarten, Helen Bouvier, Richard J. Copello, Martha Cedar, Homer Dalbey, Robert P. Farrell, Donald A. Franks, Richard B, Hadley, Wesley R. Harkins, Donald Hayden, David Kiely, Mike Lamm, Royce Saunders, Bob Sederholm, Gary Sherrard, T. R. Swennes, T. A. Wiedemann, and Frank B. Wood.

Several persons generously support a fund at San Francisco State University that supports old truck research. We acknowledge some of the donors: Stuart B. Abraham, Phillip S. Baumgarten, Edward C. Couderc, of Sausalito Moving & Storage, Gene Bills, Gilbert Hall, David Kiely, ROADSHOW, Gene Olson, Oshkosh Truck Foundation, Art Van Aken, Charlie Wacker, Bill West, and Fred Woods. Several chapters of the American Truck Historical Society have also provided financial support to the program at San Francisco State University. The chapters include: Black Swamp, Central Coast of California, Hiawathaland, Inland Empire, Mason-Dixon, Metro Jersey, Minnesota Metro, Music City, Northeast Ohio, Shenandoah Valley, and Southern Michigan.

Donald F. Wood

San Francisco State University
December 1998

A 1919 White with American Railway Express markings delivering an auto in New York City. CREDIT: Volvo/White

INTRODUCTION

New cars and trucks, once they were built, had to be delivered to customers. Rail was, and still is, the most common method of delivery although at the end of the rail haul a truck-trailer is used to make deliveries to dealers. This book devotes most of its space to these trucks, but it is important to remember that other modes of transport were used as well. During the entire century, the nation's road system was being developed. In the early days of the auto industry only railroads could be used for dependable intercity movements.

Not all cars would go directly to dealers. In the early days many car bodies were "custom-built" so the chassis would be delivered first to the body builder who would complete the auto and then deliver it to the customer. Today many truck bodies are built and installed by body manufacturers in their shops; and the completed truck is then delivered.

There are a number of ways the auto can be delivered to the customer. The simplest is to have the buyer pick it up at the plant. A small number of people do this. In 1955, the author took a plant tour of the Oldsmobile plant in Lansing and on the same tour trams were several couples who had traveled to Lansing to pick up their new Oldsmobiles.

The second way to deliver new autos would be to use the "Convoy" system with a group of drivers, each in a separate new car, driving to a dealer and then either driving back to the plant in one auto, or taking the train. In the World War I era, Henry Ford expected dealers within 100 miles to supply drivers to pick up the autos. (The F. J. Boutell Company once hired Pullman cars so that drivers in an 80 car convoy who had driven Buicks to Columbus could return to Detroit and be ready to drive in another convoy.) In the 1920s, one manufacturer had ten-man drive-away teams, each with a captain and a mechanic. A disadvantage of drive-aways was minor road damage to the autos. Homer Dalbey, a friend of mine, spent several summers after World War II driving new Oldsmobiles from Lansing to his Uncle's dealership in Indiana. His Uncle would assemble four or five drivers and drive them to Lansing where they would each get a new car to drive back. Dalbey said the trip back was two days

because highways were not as good as those we have today, and because of the new autos' low "break-in" speeds.

Phil Hamilton has pictures of his Father's fleet in Los Angeles in 1937. At one end of the photo was a Harley-Davidson tricycle that seated two, plus its driver. Hamilton wrote: "In early days local deliveries were made by two men driving a car each . . . to the dealership, while one followed with tricycle for [their] return trip."

As highways improved, trucks were substituted for drive-away fleets. Many are pictured in this book. Similar rigs were used to make deliveries from railheads. At first there were no dimensional restrictions on highway trailers and some were gigantic. Whitehead and Kales built some flatbed trailers that were 50 feet long with an overall length of 60 feet. A company history said "No brake or side lights were considered necessary, although trailers were equipped with a tail light."

The earliest modifications of the flatbed trailer was to load the front auto so that it sloped upward, and it then occupied less of the trailer's length. Soon all cars were carried at a slope, usually between 30 and 40 degrees. This allowed five cars to be carried in the same length of trailer that could handle three loaded horizontally. The subsequent modification was to add a second deck so that two levels of autos could be carried.

In the 1930s, motorists — aided by the railroads — got state laws enacted which limited the sizes, axle spacings, and weights of trucks and truck-trailer combinations. These had immediate effects on the sizes and loads of new-car-carrying trailers. In addition, they differed from state to state so a load that was legal in one state might not be legal in another. In a Whitehead & Kales study was the photo of one trailer, known as the "Illinois Special," designed to meet the restrictions of Illinois. The trailer was first built in 1933 and carried two cars on the truck (one over the cab) and two on a tandem axle trailer, called a four wheeler, within 40-feet overall length. It was a clumsy-looking outfit, difficult to load, and a hazardous piece of equipment on the highway. When it later developed that the trailer was a semitrailer rather than a four-wheeler, it became necessary to add a "dolly" under the trailer drawbar to technically make it a four-wheeler, even though the operators chained the dolly in an "up" position while traversing other states for easier operation and to conserve the dolly tires.

Different designs of trailers were developed and most could be reconfigured in a shop to handle vehicles with different dimensions. Prior to World War II, nearly all rigs could carry four new autos; fitting on five was a challenge.

Sometimes the lower level was protected by outside walls; some rigs had the entire load covered. The full outside walls had one disadvantage, as a writer in the Boutell employee newsletter recalled; "The full sides, which were attractive in design, actually caused some problems to drivers who, when making night deliveries and the car they were unloading from the lower deck ran out of gas, were unable to move the car. Worse yet, it sometimes was impossible even to get out of the car and, on occasion, the driver was obliged to wait until morning for someone to appear and provide gasoline to operate the car."

Often one sees pictures of the top front car on a load protected by a tarpaulin. At the time when new auto models were being introduced, the loads would be completely shrouded to help build the buyers' suspense. Introduction of new auto models always placed a strain on the carriers, since the manufacturers wanted autos to be in the dealers' showroom by the introductory date. Cars going to the most distant dealer were shipped first; and haul-away firms would lease equipment to each other to help each other meet their manufacturer's shipping schedules. Sometimes new auto models required major modifications of trailers. "One auto hauler had to convert 250 trailers by cutting them in half and welding a two-foot extension in the center to take care of the 1955 model car he hauls."

Sometimes it was necessary to slightly alter the dimensions of the auto so that more could be carried. Length could be reduced by removing bumpers. A device was also developed that would compress an auto's springs so that its height would be lowered. Trailers came equipped with four ratchet tie-downs for each auto carried. Those with moving decks also required hydraulic lifts.

Railroads were another method of shipping new autos. Special boxcars were developed that had bracing racks inside which allowed the first autos loaded in each end to be raised so that one or two autos could be placed below. However, as the nation's highway system improved after World War II, railroads lost much of their new car traffic to highway carriers.

One last alternative that Ford, and eventually some of his larger competitors adopted, was to set up assembly plants at other sites. At the time of the Model-T, some Ford employees experimented with loading railcars with Ford parts. They discovered that the rail car that could hold four assembled Ford Ts could hold sufficient parts to assemble 26 Ts. Ford had the most assembly plants, although the Ford buyer was always charged "freight from Detroit." Hadley Auto Transport, a major new car carrier based in Santa Ana, California, got its start in 1931 with the name Arizona Truckaway, carrying new Fords from the Ford assembly plant in Long Beach.

Some new cars and trucks were shipped by water. On the Great Lakes some vessels carried new cars exclusively while other lake vessels, already filled with bulk cargo, would take on autos as "deck" cargo to pick up some extra revenue. Some Great Lakes vessels that carried bulk materials usually traveled on the return leg "light" (or empty); they also would carry new cars on their decks. Great Lakes commerce figures for 1928 indicate that 325,000 tons of autos were shipped at Great Lakes ports, over 70 percent from Detroit. Major receiving ports, in descending order of tonnage, were: Cleveland, Buffalo, Milwaukee, Duluth-Superior, and Green Bay. New autos were also carried on barges that moved along the Mississippi River and its tributaries, movements that continued well past World War II.

During World War II shipments of new cars were halted. Everett W. Otto, who was working for F. J. Boutell, described the industry's war efforts this way:

Auto haulers of long standing (Boutell had its beginning in 1914) had converted their tractor and trailer equipment to meet the transportation demands of the government. The trailers used for transporting automobiles were disassembled by taking off the car hauling decks. Special runways were built into the lower deck area for the transporting of gun carriages and other movable ordnance material. Some were used for transporting aircraft wings. Some were completely taken apart and then rebuilt as buses for transporting [war workers] . . . .

Much of Boutell's traffic at this time was in the driving of Army . . . trucks from the factories in Pontiac and Detroit to ports of embarkation such as Boston, New York, Baltimore, Norfolk and New Orleans. The vehicles were usually dispatched in convoys of ten at a time.

One trained driver was designated as the convoy leader. He was charged with the supervision over the other nine drivers and was responsible for the highway and bridge tolls, motel expenses, fuel for the driven trucks — and for making certain that the convoy reached the port at the time designated. . .

It was no easy task being a leader because many of the drivers in the convoy were not professional operators but were usually any citizen who had a proper driving license and could spare the time for a three-day trip. Many school teachers drove after school on Friday in a convoy to the east coast and then flew home in time for school opening on Monday. Other drivers used frequently were off-duty policemen and firemen. At a terminal that Boutell operated in Schenectady, a group of Red Cross volunteer ladies worked as a team to drive army trucks for us.

Prior to World War II, there was also domestic ocean-going freight service along our ocean coasts. For example, Ford had an assembly plant in Richmond, California, and new Fords were distributed to Los Angeles, Portland, and Seattle by water.

New trucks were also delivered by all the means described so far. Larger trucks would often go in convoys with one or two riding piggyback. Light trucks went in auto-carrying trailers. Howard Jacobson, who worked as owner-operator for Kenosha Auto Transport, delivered International pickups from the IH plant in Springfield, Ohio. A common run would be to Pomona, where his trailer could be converted to a flatbed, and he would take Wayne sweepers as a backhaul. Jacobson recalled that the loads of five pickups were very high.

> It was difficult to keep the load under 13' 6", which created problems at underpasses. On many occasions I had to back out from under a low underpass, and figure out a different route. We had cab covers we used to protect the roofs of the trucks, but low tree limbs, and other obstacles still took their toll. Also clearances between loaded vehicles were very close, and if a tie-down chain let go, one had serious loss and damage to contend with.

The federal Transportation Act of 1958 removed some of the regulatory constraints on railroads and they were able to recapture much of their new auto traffic. Automobile design at this time also helped railroads since new autos were so long that new car carriers were often forced to carry one less car per trip. The low heights of the autos allowed railroads to develop triple-deck railcars which, at first, were open on the side and then covered with fiberglass to reduce problems of vandalism. At about the same time, railroads also developed more "piggyback" traffic, truck-trailers travelling on rail flatcars. New autos traveled in this manner, with the major haul performed by the rail carriers with the short trip at the end performed by trucks. At this time, rail rates for carrying new cars dropped to about half the motor carrier rates. Many truckers dropped out of business (the writer recalls unemployed new car truck drivers picketing Wisconsin's capitol in Madison protesting loss of traffic — and jobs — to the railroads). Most new car deliveries on Great Lakes vessels also ended at about this time, also because of low rail rates.

In the mid-1970s, a new auto carrier who served a GM plant in Kansas City described the railroads' recapture of the business this way: "We used to haul to 26 states out of Kansas City. Now we rail cars to Denver, Salt Lake City and Oklahoma City and then we shuttle them out from those points [by truck] for an average 250 or 300 mile haul." Everett Otto estimated that the new car carrier industry in 1974 consisted of 50 firms running about 10,000 trucks. In the early 1950s, there had been 150 firms operating about 25,000 trucks.

In following the development of the autos, it would appear that the carrier was always expected to deliver whatever size of auto the manufacturer chose to produce. However, Lee Iacocca once said that the length of the Chrysler "K" car was determined by the number that could be carried inside a standard auto-carrying railcar.

Some autos and trucks were exported aboard ocean-going ships. Often they would be crated to reduce their bulk (since ocean rates gave preference to cargoes that were denser than a conventional auto sitting on four tires). Foreign-built cars are imported into the United States on ships that carry nothing but new autos (some carry several thousand at one time). This has provided considerable business for both truckers and railroads and actually provides "backhaul" traffic for new car carrying equipment.

Metz automobiles were manufactured in Waltham, Massachusetts. This circa-1914 model is being delivered on a horse-drawn wagon. It may be new or it may be part of an endurance run (note number on radiator). CREDIT: American Automobile Manufacturers Assn.

An atypical delivery. CREDIT: American Automobile Manufacturers Assn.

A circa-1917 Duplex truck, with four-wheel drive, carrying a load of Reo autos from Lansing to Tonawanda, New York. The front auto rides on truck's frame; rear auto rides on a four-wheel trailer. CREDIT: American Automobile Manufacturers Assn.

World War I vintage Internationals moving via highway from Akron to Philadelphia. Sign on side says: "Highway Deliveries Reduce Railroad Congestion." (Railroad congestion, especially at East Coast ports, was a major problem during World War I, and the federal government had to take over railroad operations.) CREDIT: Navistar Archives

11

Loading a single auto onto a Mack Bulldog, circa-1917. CREDIT: Mack Museum

This is a Service truck, built in Wabash, Indiana, about 1919. It's knocked down and crated for export shipment. CREDIT: Wabash County Historical Museum

A load of Ford Model T autos. The Fruehauf trailer had curtains on its side. CREDIT: Fruehauf Division

Some 1925 Moon automobiles, built in St. Louis, Missouri, being loaded on the deck of a barge in St. Louis, where they will be carried to St. Paul, Minnesota. CREDIT: American Automobile Manufacturers Assn.

A mid-1920s GMC tractor with a load of five autos. Note headlights on truck's cowl. CREDIT: American Trucking Associations

This early 1920s photo shows two Fruehauf semi-trailers moving by rail from Detroit to Des Moines on a rail flatcar. Trailers have solid rubber tires. CREDIT: Freuhaf Division

Here are a half-dozen late 1920s Internationals, if you count the tractor. For a brief period there were no length limits on highway loads, but in the 1930s motorists and railroads were able to control truck weights and dimensions. This picture was taken in Indiana. CREDIT: Pullman Trailmobile

This is the Oakland Motor Car Co. plant in Pontiac, Michigan in the late 1920s. The people on the right (including some women) are drivers waiting to drive convoys of new Oaklands to dealers. CREDIT: Baker Library, Harvard University

Loading Oakland autos aboard railcars, circa-1927. CREDIT: Baker Library, Harvard University

A straight rig from the late 1920s. Truck may be a GMC. CREDIT: Whitehead & Kales

Some 1928 Chevrolet autos and one panel truck being pulled by a GMC operated by Nicholson Transportation of Stratford, New Jersey. CREDIT: Pullman Trailmobile

A crated Mack truck from the late 1920s. CREDIT: Mack Museum

CREDIT: Mack Museum

CREDIT: Mack Museum

A load of 1929 Nash autos.
CREDIT: Pullman Trailmobile

A Noble truck pulling a load of 1929 Auburns on a long flat-bed trailer. What would that load be worth today? CREDIT: American Automobile Manufacturers Assn.

Two pairs of White trucks, starting out as a convoy, circa-1929.
CREDIT: Volvo/White

A Ford AA with an extremely long frame and a long trailer, with a load of 1931 Ford model As. CREDIT: Convoy Company

An early modification of the long flatbed trailer. The ramp at the front tips rearward to load auto. CREDIT: Pullman Trailmobile

Then it tips up, once the auto is loaded. CREDIT: Pullman Trailmobile

A circa-1930 White with a load of new autos. The slogan across top of windshield says, "We save the first mileage." This truck has New York plates. CREDIT: Volvo/White

This tractor is an early 1930s
Dodge. CREDIT: Detroit Trailer

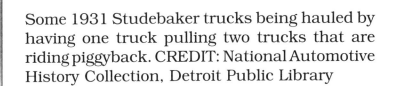

Some 1931 Studebaker trucks being hauled by
having one truck pulling two trucks that are
riding piggyback. CREDIT: National Automotive
History Collection, Detroit Public Library

A 1932 Buick on a GMC flatbed. CREDIT: National Automotive History Collection, Detroit Public Library

Two 1932 Studebaker trucks and what is probably a Studebaker auto, in 1932. CREDIT: National Automotive History Collection, Detroit Public Library

Some 1932 Chevrolets. The tractor is also a Chevrolet, circa-1930. CREDIT: Anchor Motor Freight, Inc.

An early 1930s GMC operated by Boutell. The rear car on top is a 1933-1934 Ford. CREDIT: Whitehead & Kales

Some 1933 Chevrolets. The tractor is a GMC of similar vintage. CREDIT: Anchor Motor Freight, Inc.

A Ford truck with a long frame pulling a long trailer. Tarpaulins are hoisted along the sides. CREDIT: Oregon Historical Society

Some 1933-1934 Fords being unloaded from haul-away trailers and then loaded aboard a ship. At the top of the ship, is a large "FORD" sign, hinting that this vessel may also have been Ford-owned. CREDIT: American Automobile Manufacturers Assn.

A fleet of Fords operated by Consolidated Convoy Company in Portland, Oregon, in 1933. CREDIT: Oregon Historical Society

A 1933-1934 Ford truck with three 1935 Fords - one on the truck and two on a trailer. CREDIT: Hadley Auto Transport

Two 1933 Indiana trucks with California plates. The grille of the rear truck is protected by heavy paper. CREDIT: Volvo/White

A 1934-1935 Chevrolet operated by Howard Sober, Inc., of Lansing, Michigan, with a load of 1935 Oldsmobiles. Note their bumpers are not yet attached. When the author was a small boy, his Father drove a 1935 Olds like the one on the right. CREDIT: Whitehead & Kales

These three 1934 Chevrolet sedan deliveries are being delivered to Anheuser-Busch, where they will be used by salesmen for yeast and malt syrup. The truck tractor is a 1933 Ford. CREDIT: Automobile Transport, Inc.

Three 1934 DeSoto airflows waiting to be loaded. The truck tractors are Dodges. CREDIT: Chrysler Historical Collection

The Baker Haulaway Company ran this circa-1934 Dodge with a Whitehead & Kales body. CREDIT: Whitehead & Kales

Making believe that his trailer is being pulled by a team of horses. CREDIT: Anchor Motor Freight, Inc.

The sides enclosing this trailer are being pulled by a Dodge tractor. The autos are 1934 Plymouths, and the sign in rear window of the one on the right says its price is $495. CREDIT: Fruehauf Division

"Lightering" an ocean vessel means transferring cargo to and from land using a small boat or barge. This 1935 Dodge is shown being lightered off the coast of Peru. CREDIT: American Automobile Manufacturers Assn.

Two mid-1930s Internationals riding aboard a ship on their way to the Yukon. CREDIT: Navistar Archives

Some 1935 Packards being driven off a Great Lakes vessel that operated between Detroit and Buffalo. CREDIT: American Automobile Manufacturers Assn.

A mid-1930s Dodge with a Whitehead & Kales frame and trailer. The rear wheels on truck do not match; possibly, the rear axle's dolly also functions as a dolly for trailer. CREDIT: Whitehead & Kales

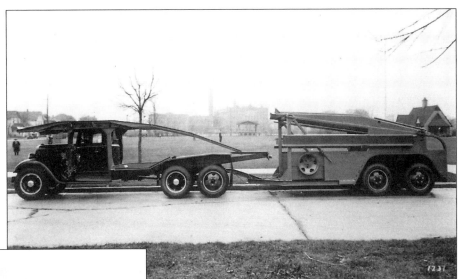

F. J. Boutell used this Whitehead & Kales equipment carried by a mid-1930s Dodge. CREDIT: Whitehead & Kales

A fleet of 1935 Ford haulaway trucks in front of a Ford plant. The slogan painted on side says, "Watch the Fords go by." CREDIT: National Automotive History Collection, Detroit Public Library

A 1935 Ford, operated by Walsh Auto Transportation, pulling a completely enclosed Whitehead & Kales trailer. CREDIT: Whitehead & Kales

A fleet of Ford flatbeds in 1935, with uniformed drivers in front. CREDIT: Hadley Auto Transport

Unloading a 1936 Buick in Los Angeles, California.
CREDIT: Southern Pacific

CREDIT: Southern Pacific

A 1936 Ford pulling two Lincoln sedans. CREDIT: Convoy Company

A 1936 White tractor pulling a White flatbed and a Packard 120. Wheels are removed from the flatbed truck to allow it to pivot around the fifth wheel. CREDIT: Volvo/White

Some 1937 Chevrolets, crated for export, being lightered (transferred) from a barge onto an ocean-going vessel in New York harbor. CREDIT: Baker Library, Harvard University

New 1937 Chryslers at the end of the assembly line. In the rear of the photo we can see the waiting rail cars and the parked autos waiting to be loaded. CREDIT: Chrysler Historical Collection

A 1937 Chevrolet being weighed on scales. After being weighed, it would pull forward and the trailer would be weighed. CREDIT: Complete Auto Transit, Inc.

An auto-carrying rack built by Whitehead & Kales on a 1937 Chevrolet. CREDIT: Whitehead & Kales

A trailerload of 1937 Packards. CREDIT: Whitehead & Kales

A 1937 Ford tractor with a Whitehead & Kales trailer. CREDIT: Whitehead & Kales

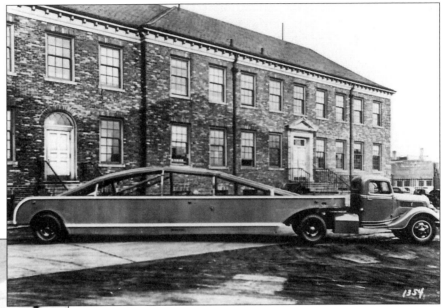

A 1937 Ford carrying some 1939-1940 Ford products. CREDIT: Hadley Auto Transport

The front of this 1937 Lincoln has been lifted on the rack inside the rail car so that another auto can be placed below. Tag on grilles says radiator has been drained, and tag near person's hand says the same about the crankcase. CREDIT: Southern Pacific

Two Studebaker trucks, each carrying a 1937 Studebaker auto. CREDIT: Antique Studebaker Club

A pair of 1937 Studebakers with the one in front pulling. Note covering over front of truck being pulled. CREDIT: Antique Studebaker Club

Two views of a trailer with an enclosed bottom, built by Whitehead & Kales. The sides provided space for advertising signs. The tractor is a customized Chevrolet. CREDIT: Whitehead & Kales

Barely visible below the "k" in the word "Buick" on the side of the truck, is a small door. CREDIT: Whitehead & Kales

Lifting a 1938 Hudson aboard an ocean-going ship. CREDIT: Baker Library, Harvard University

This drawing shows the interior of a new car carrying rail boxcar. Note how upper cars are angled to provide space below. CREDIT: American Automobile Manufacturers Assn.

Here's a cooperative venture involving new White trucks and Packard autos, circa 1938. CREDIT: Volvo/White

A 1939 Chevrolet COE pulling a Whitehead & Kales trailer which the firm referred to as a "humpback 3-truck 3-car trailer." CREDIT: Whitehead & Kales

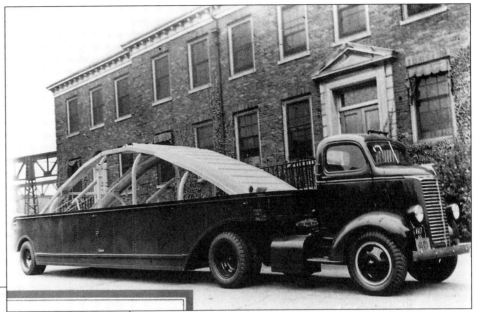

A Boutell 1939 Chevrolet with a load of 1940 Buicks. The autos lack front bumpers–they were installed after delivery. CREDIT: Library of Congress

A 1939 Ford COE delivering a Ford chassis with cab and a Ford pickup. CREDIT: National Automotive History Collection, Detroit Public Library

Some 1939 Ford tractors with Whitehead & Kales trailers. CREDIT: Whitehead & Kales

A 1939 Ford, operated by Arizona Truck-A-Way, with a load of 1941 Ford products. CREDIT: Hadley Auto Transport

A 1939 Ford with a load of Ford trucks and a Mercury automobile. CREDIT: Oregon Historical Society

Shipping cabs and boxes of 1939 Studebakers by rail to an assembly plant. CREDIT: American Automobile Manufacturers Assn.

View inside a Whitehead & Kales trailer, circa 1939. Rear of upper deck is in raised position. CREDIT: Whitehead & Kales

Loading a 1939 White stepvan (White Horse) aboard a vessel. CREDIT: Volvo/White

A 1941 Chevrolet, photographed in 1943 with a load of army trucks. CREDIT: Library of Congress

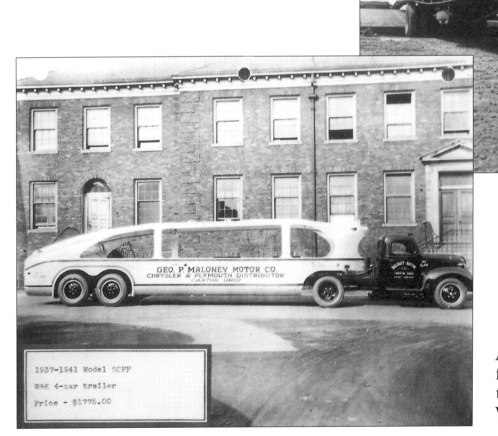

1937-1941 Model SCFP
W&K 4-car trailer
Price – $1775.00

A Whitehead & Kales 4-car trailer, produced from 1937 to 1941, selling for $1775. The tractor is a circa-1940 Dodge. CREDIT: Whitehead & Kales

A 1941 Chevrolet, transporting three others. CREDIT: Complete Auto Transit, Inc.

Some 1941 Ford autos and light trucks. The tractor is a late 1930's Ford. CREDIT: Oregon Historical Society

A load of 1941 Buicks. CREDIT: Baker Library, Harvard University

Not new car carriers, but close, are these trailer bodies, used for carrying nearly-completed auto bodies to a plant where they would be placed on chassis. These bodies are for 1941 Cadillacs. The truck on the left is a 1940 Chevrolet; on the right, a 1937. CREDIT: American Automobile Manufacturers Assn.

Staging 1941 Plymouths by railcars into which they will be loaded. Some have the rear bumper disassembled. CREDIT: Chrysler Historical Collection

Loading 1942 Chevrolets aboard a railcar. CREDIT: Southern Pacific

A rig operated by F. J. Boutell carrying some wartime cargo. The tractor is probably a GMC. Note the jeep above cab. CREDIT: American Trucking Associations

A World War II load carried by Boutell. The tractor is a Chevrolet. Does its driver see the large gun in his rear-view mirror? CREDIT: F. J. Boutell

In this picture, the auto-carrying racks are not in use and are stowed at the top of this railcar. The Army truck could have been backed in and later pushed, or driven, forward. CREDIT: Southern Pacific

Some 1946 Chevrolets being carried by Pacific Motor Transport (PMT), a subsidiary of the Southern Pacific Railroad. CREDIT: Southern Pacific

This Chevrolet tractor has no chrome, it's probably from 1942. Its load does have chrome; they're probably 1946 models. CREDIT: Southern Pacific

Three 1946 Buicks on a Boutell rig. The tractor is a 1942 Chevrolet. CREDIT: F. J. Boutell

A completely enclosed Boutell trailer pulled by a 1940's Dodge tractor. CREDIT: F. J. Boutell

A load of 1946 Nash autos, being carried by Kenosha Auto Transport. Nash autos were built in Kenosha. The tractor is an International. CREDIT: Whitehead & Kales

66

Four 1947 Studebakers. The tractor is a
Dodge. CREDIT: National Archives

Four 1947 Lincolns. The tractor is an early 1940s
Ford. CREDIT: Automobile Transport Inc.

Two bargeloads of mainly 1946-1948 GM products and a few Chrysler products travelling on triple-deck barges on the Ohio River. On the near barge are also some light trucks. CREDIT: American Automobile Manufacturers Assn.

Two makes of 1949 autos being carried on the top deck of this Great Lakes vessel: Chevrolets on the left, Hudsons on the right. CREDIT: American Automobile Manufacturers Assn.

A load of new 1949 Fords being carried by E & L Transport Company. CREDIT: Lorin Sorensen

A load of 1949 Ford autos. Two are on the truck; two are on the trailer. CREDIT: Hadley Auto Transport

Kaisers and Frazers, circa-1949. To the left we see trailers waiting to be loaded. The closest tractor to us is a Chevrolet COE. CREDIT: American Automobile Manufacturers Assn.

In 1949 Oldsmobiles came with a "hot" new V-8 engine. Here are some used to promote a 500-mile race. The truck tractor is a 1948 GMC cabover, operated by Howard Sober, Inc., of Lansing, Michigan. CREDIT: American Automobile Manufacturers Assn.

Some 1949-1950 Crosleys being carried two abreast on a Kenosha Auto Transport rig, pulled by an International. CREDIT: American Automobile Manufacturers Assn.

Loading a circa-1950 Oshkosh truck aboard an aircraft. The wheels have been removed. CREDIT: Oshkosh Truck Corporation

This circa-1950 Dodge COE tractor was rebuilt so the cab would be so far above the engine that the front of the auto could be stowed. The third axle from the left is a trailer dolly. CREDIT: Phill Baumgarten

A 1950 Lincoln being carried above a truck's cab. Note the truck's two spare tires and water bag hanging behind man on right. CREDIT: Hadley Auto Transport

Large farm tractors and implements had cargo characteristics similar to autos. Here, an early 1950s International with a flatbed trailer delivers a load of IH Farmall tractors. The trucker was based in Grand Island, Nebraska. CREDIT: American Automobile Manufacturers Assn.

Treolar Trucking Co., operating in the Midwest, sealed the bottoms of its car-carrying trailers so they could carry backhauls of grain. This rig, with a circa-1950 White tractor, is unloading grain at an elevator. CREDIT: American Automobile Manufacturers Assn.

An early 1950s White Freightliner car carrier with a backhaul of lumber. The transportation regulations in effect at that time made it difficult for carriers to contract to carry "backhauls." CREDIT: Phill Baumgarten

A 1952 White tractor, operated by Bolin Drive-A-Way Co., with a load of 1952 Studebakers. Note tarps on top cars.
CREDIT: Volvo/White

This is the loading dock operated by the Nicholson Transit Co. Cars nearby are 1953 Chryslers. CREDIT: American Truck Historical Society

The upper two decks of this Great Lakes vessel are carrying 1954 Plymouths. A loading ramp is visible on far right. CREDIT Wesley R. Harkins

This Hadley Auto Transport rig has apparently just been picked at the trailer builder's shop; the pickup truck the driver used to reach the shop is now being carried back. CREDIT: Hadley Auto Transport

Double deck rail cars on parallel tracks carrying 1954 Buicks on the right and International pickups on the left.
CREDIT: Southern Pacific

A mid-1950s Ford tractor pulling a load consisting of a Jeep, some Studebakers, and Mercurys. The sleeper cab is unusual for a haulaway rig since the space was normally needed for cargo, especially in this era of very large cars. CREDIT: Convoy Company

A Convoy Company C-series Ford with a load of 1957 Ford products. CREDIT: Convoy Company

A Kenosha Auto Transport's 1956 GMC with a load of Nash autos. CREDIT: National Archives

Some late 1950s GMC trucks on a trailer. CREDIT: Complete Auto Transit

Some late 1950s Chrysler products. Note their length. Above the truck's cab are racks for another auto, but insufficient length for carrying it. CREDIT: Complete Auto Transit, Inc.

A 1958 Freightliner with a load of 1958 Chrysler products, including some Imperials. CREDIT: Freightliner Corp.

Some 1958 Dodges being carried as "deck" cargo aboard a Great Lakes vessel. The vessel may also be carrying some bulk commodity such as limestone or grain in its holds. CREDIT: Wesley R. Harkins

A load of 1959 Chevrolets carried by PMT. The tractor is a GMC.
CREDIT: Whitehead & Kales

A Ford C-series tractor, operated by the Convoy Company, with a load of Dodge army trucks. CREDIT: American Truck Historical Society

Loading jeeps aboard a tri-level auto-carrying railcar using a scissors-lift mounted on a 1959 International chassis. CREDIT: Hockensmith Corp.

A late 1950s Ford with a load of circa-1960 Chrysler products. CREDIT: Complete Auto Transit

Unloading some "Forward Control" Jeeps, circa-1960. CREDIT: American Automobile Manufacturers Assn.

This 1960 photo shows the ramps (known as "skids") set for loading the lower deck of the trailer. Barely visible behind the truck cab is a hydraulic piston used to adjust the tilt of the upper front deck. CREDIT: Southern Pacific

A batch of one-way rental trailers being carried "home" on a new-car carrying trailer. CREDIT: Phill Baumgarten

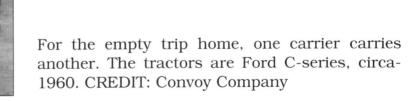

For the empty trip home, one carrier carries another. The tractors are Ford C-series, circa-1960. CREDIT: Convoy Company

An elevator for lifting autos so they can be loaded or unloaded from multi-deck rail cars. This photo was taken at a Southern Pacific rail yard. The auto is a Cadillac. CREDIT: B. F. Goodrich Collection, Univ. of Akron Archives

This early 1960s picture shows 946 trucks leaving Springfield, Ohio, the "largest drive-away in International Truck history". CREDIT: American Automobile Manufacturers Assn.

This is a piggyback operation with the truck trailer load of early 1960s Corvairs carried on a rail flat car. Once the train reached its destination, the trailer would be attached to a truck tractor, which would then make deliveries to dealers. CREDIT: Southern Pacific

A load of Chevrolets in the mid-1960s leaving the plant at Flint, Michigan. The truck, also a Chevrolet, has Michigan plates, and was operated by Anchor Motor Freight. The device above auto checks for height clearance. CREDIT: Chevrolet

This mid-1960s Ford Mustang is being loaded aboard a United Airlines freighter. CREDIT: American Trucking Associations

Some late 1960s Macks travelling piggyback.
CREDIT: Mack

Loading a large shipment of Mack trucks aboard an ocean vessel. CREDIT: Mack

The Convoy Company used this as a test load of a full truck (carrying three autos) pulling two loaded trailers (carrying six and four autos, respectively). The tractor is a 1967 Ford. CREDIT: Convoy Company

Railcars on five sets of tracks carrying late 1960s Internationals from Springfield, Ohio to Houston. Many of the trucks were recreational vehicles and were used to stock a local sales campaign. CREDIT: American Automobile Manufacturers Assn.

Seven Cadillacs carried on an Anchor rig, pulled by a 1970 Chevrolet tractor. In this era Cadillacs were probably the largest autos to be handled. CREDIT: Anchor Motor Freight, Inc.

These Cadillacs are being loaded three high into containers which will be lifted aboard rail flatcars. In the rear are triple-deck rail cars. CREDIT: Southern Pacific

These railcars (with a trade name called Vert-A-Pac) carried compact autos tipped on end. Inside the railcar we see autos riding at 90-degree angles. Thirty Vegas could be carried in a single railcar. CREDIT: Southern Pacific

A loading dock at a Chevrolet plant in the early 1970s. CREDIT: Anchor Motor Freight, Inc.

An early 1970s Dodge cab-over with a load of 13 Ford Pintos. CREDIT: Convoy Company

An early 1970s GMC, operated by Nu-Car Carriers, carrying a mixed load of ten intermediate-size autos. CREDIT: Nu-Car Carriers

A load of eight early 1970s Chevrolet Vegas. The trailer has 1973 Ohio plates and was operated by Anchor Motor Freight. CREDIT: Anchor Motor Freight, Inc.

This mid-1970s Ford is pulling a mixed load of autos, a pickup truck, a van, and farm tractors. CREDIT: Convoy Company

A mid-1970s Ford, operated by Nu-Car Carriers, carrying a load of Fords. CREDIT: Nu-Car Carriers

A late 1970s Ford with seven autos. Note length of auto over the truck's cab. CREDIT: Nu-Car Carriers

A mid-1970s GMC carrying some 1990s Mitsubishi autos. CREDIT: Richard J. Copello

Interior view of the Convoy Company's shop in Portland, Oregon. The trailer on right is being reconfigured to handle a certain size of auto. CREDIT: Convoy Company

A Boeing 747 with a load of Ford Tempos and a Mercury Topaz. Note the Tempo banner - this must be at the time of the Tempo line's introduction. The elaborate ramp might be a car carrying trailer. CREDIT: Northwest Orient Airlines

A Peterbilt, from the early 1980s, with a load of Renaults.
CREDIT: Richard J. Copello

A Leaseway Ford tractor from the early 1980s with a load of Ford and Mercury products. CREDIT: Richard J. Copello

Both Ford and GM products are on this mid-1980s GMC.
CREDIT: Richard J. Copello

A late 1980s GMC unloading Chrysler products in front of dealer. CREDIT: Richard J. Copello

A late 1980s International run by T. Berry Auto Transport. CREDIT: Richard J. Copello

An early 1990s GMC with a load of Dodge Colts. CREDIT: Richard J. Copello

A circa-1992 Freightliner with a load of mid 1990s Fords. CREDIT: Richard J. Copello

A circa-1993 Freightliner. Note the raised tow-bar in front. CREDIT: Richard J. Copello

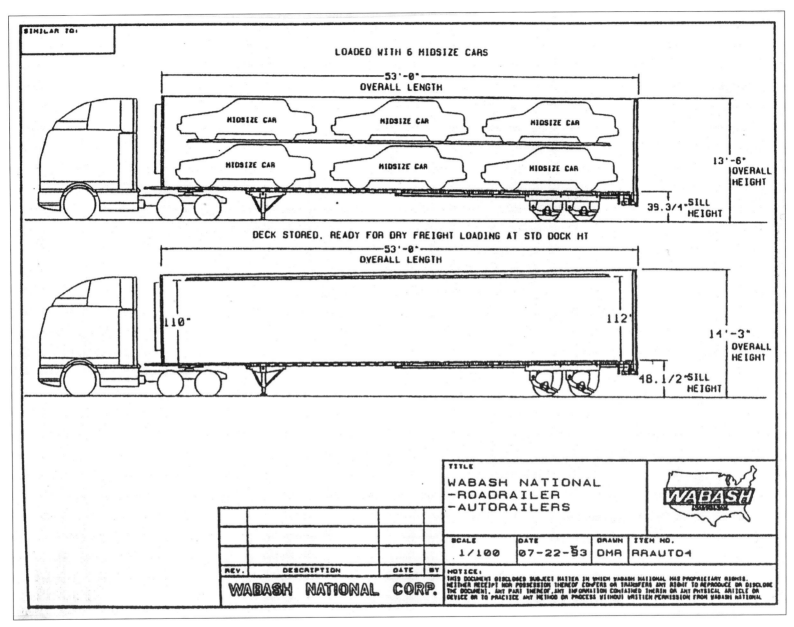

"Roadrailer" trailers can operate on the highways and also have rail wheels so that strings of them can move on rail tracks. This diagram shows the design of one with a stowable auto-carrying deck. CREDIT: Roadrailer Division, Wabash National Corporation.

References

"Automobile Haulers Respond to Changing Business Needs," The Kansas Transporter, October, 1976, pp. 8-13.

"Autos Loaded at Angle in Auto Trailer to Save Space," Popular Mechanics, September, 1930, p. 366.

H. V. Collins "High-Lights in the Development of Auto-Transport Trailers," prepared for Whitehead & Kales Company, 1942.

Fruehauf Trailer Company literature, circa 1955.

Phil Hamilton, "Pioneer New Car Hauling in the West," Wheels of Time, Vol.8, No. 2, (March/April, 1987), pp. 10-13.

Howard Jacobson, "Kenosha Auto Transport," Wheels of Time, Vol.19, No. 3, (May/June, 1998), pp. 18-19.

Mechanical Handling Systems, Inc. literature, circa 1955.

Allan Nevins, Ford: The Times, The Man, The Company (New York: Charles Scribner's Sons, 1954).

Everett W. Otto, "Boutell — Pioneer Auto Transporter," Wheels of Time, Vol. 3, No. 1, (1982), pp. 14-17.

————, "Forty-five years of oil and cars," AOT News, October-December, 1974, pp. 12-15, 27.

Stuart Trailer literature, circa 1965.

Tell-A-Bout (employee newspaper of the F. J. Boutell Driveaway Co., Inc,) several issues, 1976.

"$250,000,000 Giant," TDA News Vol. 23, No. 1, (1955), pp. 3-5.

U. S. Army Corps of Engineers, Transportation on the Great Lakes (Washington, D.C.: Government Printing Office, 1930).

Whitehead & Kales Co. literature, circa 1950.

Donald F. Wood, "Convoy Carriers," Special-Interest Autos, No. 41 (1977), pp. 46-51.

————, "Early Trucks Were Delivered by Rail, Sea, Air, and all Manner of Highway Modes," Wheels of Time, Vol. 1, No. 2, (1980) pp. 14-16.

More Titles from Iconografix:

AMERICAN CULTURE

AMERICAN SERVICE STATIONS 1935-1943
ISBN 1-882256-27-1
COCA-COLA: A HISTORY IN PHOTOGRAPHS 1930-1969
ISBN 1-882256-46-8
COCA-COLA: ITS VEHICLES IN PHOTOGRAPHS 1930-1969
ISBN 1-882256-47-6
PHILLIPS 66 1945-1954 ISBN 1-882256-42-5

AUTOMOTIVE

CADILLAC 1948-1964 ISBN 1-882256-83-2
CORVETTE PROTOTYPES & SHOW CARS
ISBN 1-882256-77-8
EARLY FORD V-8S 1932-1942 ISBN 1-882256-97-2
FERRARI PININFARINA 1952-1996 ISBN 1-882256-65-4
IMPERIAL 1955-1963 ISBN 1-882256-22-0
IMPERIAL 1964-1968 ISBN 1-882256-23-9
LINCOLN MOTOR CARS 1920-1942 ISBN 1-882256-57-3
LINCOLN MOTOR CARS 1946-1960 ISBN 1-882256-58-1
PACKARD MOTOR CARS 1935-1942 ISBN 1-882256-44-1
PACKARD MOTOR CARS 1946-1958 ISBN 1-882256-45-X
PONTIAC DREAM CARS, SHOW CARS & PROTOTYPES
1928-1998 ISBN 1-882256-93-X
PONTIAC FIREBIRD TRANS-AM 1969-1999
ISBN 1-882256-95-6
PORSCHE 356 1948-1965 ISBN 1-882256-85-9
STUDEBAKER 1933-1942 ISBN 1-882256-24-7
STUDEBAKER 1946-1958 ISBN 1-882256-25-5

EMERGENCY VEHICLES

AMERICAN LAFRANCE 700 SERIES 1945-1952
ISBN 1-882256-90-5
AMERICAN LAFRANCE 700&800 SERIES 1953-1958
ISBN 1-882256-91-3
CLASSIC AMERICAN AMBULANCES 1900-1998
ISBN 1-882256-94-8
FIRE CHIEF CARS 1900-1997 ISBN 1-882256-87-5
MACK MODEL B FIRE TRUCKS 1954-1966*
ISBN 1-882256-62-X
MACK MODEL CF FIRE TRUCKS 1967-1981*
ISBN 1-882256-63-8
MACK MODEL L FIRE TRUCKS 1940-1954*
ISBN 1-882256-86-7

RACING

GT40 ISBN 1-882256-64-6

LE MANS 1950: THE BRIGGS CUNNINGHAM
CAMPAIGN ISBN 1-882256-21-2
LOLA RACE CARS 1962-1990 ISBN 1-882256-73-5
LOTUS RACE CARS 1961-1994 ISBN 1-882256-84-0
MCLAREN RACE CARS 1965-1996 ISBN 1-882256-74-3
SEBRING 12-HOUR RACE 1970 ISBN 1-882256-20-4
VANDERBILT CUP RACE 1936 & 1937
ISBN 1-882256-66-2
WILLIAMS 1969-1999 30 YEARS OF GRAND PRIX RACING
ISBN 1-58388-000-3

RAILWAYS

CHICAGO, ST. PAUL, MINNEAPOLIS & OMAHA RAILWAY
1880-1940 ISBN 1-882256-67-0
CHICAGO&NORTH WESTERN RAILWAY 1975-1995
ISBN 1-882256-76-X
GREAT NORTHERN RAILWAY 1945-1970
ISBN 1-882256-56-5
GREAT NORTHERN RAILWAY 1945-1970 VOLUME 2
ISBN 1-882256-79-4
MILWAUKEE ROAD 1850-1960 ISBN 1-882256-61-1
SOO LINE 1975-1992 ISBN 1-882256-68-9
WISCONSIN CENTRAL LIMITED 1987-1996
ISBN 1-882256-75-1
WISCONSIN CENTRAL RAILWAY 1871-1909
ISBN 1-882256-78-6

TRUCKS

BEVERAGE TRUCKS 1910-1975 ISBN 1-882256-60-3
BROCKWAY TRUCKS 1948-1961* ISBN 1-882256-55-7
DODGE PICKUPS 1939-1978 ISBN 1-882256-82-4
DODGE POWER WAGONS 1940-1980 ISBN 1-882256-89-1
DODGE TRUCKS 1929-1947 ISBN 1-882256-36-0
DODGE TRUCKS 1948-1960 ISBN 1-882256-37-9
EL CAMINO 1959-1987 INCLUDING GMC SPRINT &
CABALLERO ISBN 1-882256-92-1
LOGGING TRUCKS 1915-1970 ISBN 1-882256-59-X
MACK® MODEL AB* ISBN 1-882256-18-2
MACK AP SUPER-DUTY TRUCKS 1926-1938*
ISBN 1-882256-54-9
MACK MODEL B 1953-1966 VOL 1* ISBN 1-882256-19-0
MACK MODEL B 1953-1966 VOL 2* ISBN 1-882256-34-4
MACK EB-EC-ED-EE-EF-EG-DE 1936-1951*
ISBN 1-882256-29-8

MACK EH-EJ-EM-EQ-ER-ES 1936-1950*
ISBN 1-882256-39-5
MACK FC-FCSW-NW 1936-1947* ISBN 1-882256-28-X
MACK FG-FH-FJ-FK-FN-FP-FT-FW 1937-1950*
ISBN 1-882256-35-2
MACK LF-LH-LJ-LM-LT 1940-1956* ISBN 1-882256-38-7
MACK TRUCKS PHOTO GALLERY* ISBN 1-882256-88-3
NEW CAR CARRIERS 1910-1998 ISBN 1-882256-98-0
STUDEBAKER TRUCKS 1927-1940 ISBN 1-882256-40-9
STUDEBAKER TRUCKS 1941-1964 ISBN 1-882256-41-7
WHITE TRUCKS 1900-1937 ISBN 1-882256-80-8

TRACTORS & CONSTRUCTION EQUIPMENT

CASE TRACTORS 1912-1959 ISBN 1-882256-32-8
CATERPILLAR D-2 & R-2 ISBN 1-882256-99-9
CATERPILLAR D-8 1933-1974 INCLUDING DIESEL 75
ISBN 1-882256-96-4
CATERPILLAR MILITARY TRACTORS VOLUME 1
ISBN 1-882256-16-6
CATERPILLAR MILITARY TRACTORS VOLUME 2
ISBN 1-882256-17-4
CATERPILLAR SIXTY ISBN 1-882256-05-0
CATERPILLAR PHOTO GALLERY ISBN 1-882256-70-0
CLETRAC AND OLIVER CRAWLERS ISBN 1-882256-43-3
ERIE SHOVEL ISBN 1-882256-69-7
FARMALL CUB ISBN 1-882256-71-9
FARMALL F– SERIES ISBN 1-882256-02-6
FARMALL MODEL H ISBN 1-882256-03-4
FARMALL MODEL M ISBN 1-882256-15-8
FARMALL REGULAR ISBN 1-882256-14-X
FARMALL SUPER SERIES ISBN 1-882256-49-2
FORDSON 1917-1928 ISBN 1-882256-33-6
HART-PARR ISBN 1-882256-08-5
HOLT TRACTORS ISBN 1-882256-10-7
INTERNATIONAL TRACTRACTOR ISBN 1-882256-48-4
INTERNATIONAL TD CRAWLERS 1933-1962
ISBN 1-882256-72-7
JOHN DEERE MODEL A ISBN 1-882256-12-3
JOHN DEERE MODEL B ISBN 1-882256-01-8
JOHN DEERE MODEL D ISBN 1-882256-00-X
JOHN DEERE 30 SERIES ISBN 1-882256-13-1
MINNEAPOLIS-MOLINE U-SERIES ISBN 1-882256-07-7
OLIVER TRACTORS ISBN 1-882256-09-3
RUSSELL GRADERS ISBN 1-882256-11-5
TWIN CITY TRACTOR ISBN 1-882256-06-9

*This product is sold under license from Mack Trucks, Inc. Mack is a registered Trademark of Mack Trucks, Inc. All rights reserved.

All Iconografix books are available from direct mail specialty book dealers and bookstores worldwide, or can be ordered from the publisher. For book trade and distribution information or to add your name to our mailing list contact

Iconografix
PO Box 446
Hudson, Wisconsin, 54016

Telephone: (715) 381-9755
(800) 289-3504 (USA)
Fax: (715) 381-9756

AMERICAN SERVICE STATIONS
1935-1943 PHOTO ARCHIVE
Edited by M. Kirn

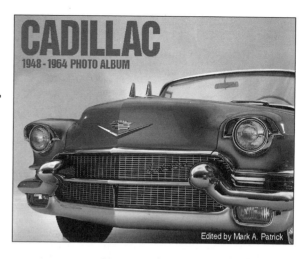

CADILLAC
1948-1964 PHOTO ALBUM
Edited by Mark A. Patrick

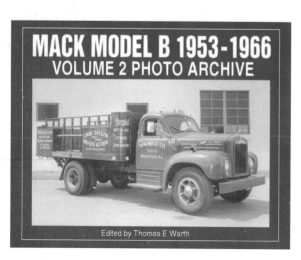

LOGGING TRUCKS
1915-1970 PHOTO ARCHIVE
Donald F. Wood

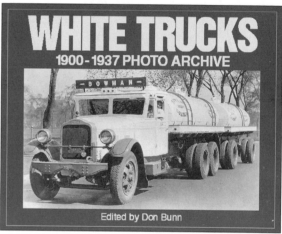

WHITE TRUCKS
1900-1937 PHOTO ARCHIVE
Edited by Don Bunn

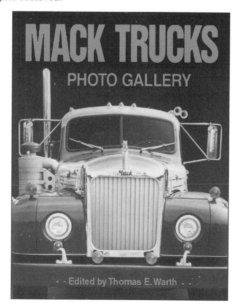

MACK TRUCKS
PHOTO GALLERY
Edited by Thomas E. Warth

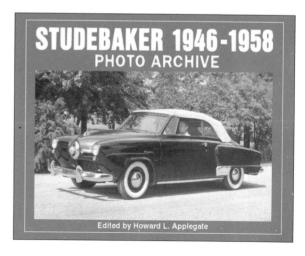

MACK MODEL B 1953-1966
VOLUME 2 PHOTO ARCHIVE
Edited by Thomas E Warth

STUDEBAKER 1946-1958
PHOTO ARCHIVE
Edited by Howard L. Applegate